A WALK
WITH
God

LOIS J. CARTER

authorHOUSE®

AuthorHouse™
1663 Liberty Drive
Bloomington, IN 47403
www.authorhouse.com
Phone: 833-262-8899

Published by AuthorHouse 09/24/2020

ISBN: 978-1-6655-0179-8 (sc)
ISBN: 978-1-6655-0178-1 (e)

Library of Congress Control Number: 2020918918

Print information available on the last page.

Any people depicted in stock imagery provided by Getty Images are models,
and such images are being used for illustrative purposes only.
Certain stock imagery © Getty Images.

This book is printed on acid-free paper.

Because of the dynamic nature of the Internet, any web addresses or links contained in this book may have changed
since publication and may no longer be valid. The views expressed in this work are solely those of the author and do
not necessarily reflect the views of the publisher, and the publisher hereby disclaims any responsibility for them.

Scripture taken from The Holy Bible, King James Version. Public Domain

A Walk with God is written for and dedicated to my loving family and to everyone involved in the struggles of life. A special thanks to my granddaughter, Carley Carter, for her assistance in completing this book.

"Thy word is a lamp unto my feet, and a light unto my path".

—Psalm 119:105

"Trust in the Lord with all thine heart and lean not unto thine own understanding. In all thy ways acknowledge him, and he shall direct thy paths".

—Proverbs 3:5–6

"And the Lord shall guide thee continually, and satisfy thy soul in drought, and make fat thy bones; and thou shalt be like a watered garden, and like a spring of water whose waters fail not".

—Isaiah 58:11

"The steps of a good man are ordered by the Lord; and he delighteth in his way. Though he fall, he shall not be utterly cast down; for the Lord upholdeth him with his hand".

—Psalm 37:23–24

CONTENTS

PREFACE

Detailed by chapter and interspersed with poetry, *A Walk with God* expresses various aspects of daily Christian living, including the challenges and triumphs that offer hope, not only in this life but also eternally.

I am thankful for my heritage, thankful for a genuine Bible experience, and thankful to know the oneness of God our Savior and soon-coming King. Pentecostals are well-known for their praise and worship. Thank God for that, but there is a personal walk that He desires to take with us, a path that each individual must find, a true relationship with Him. Jesus is the light shining across our path. He will lead us and guide us each step of the way. Exodus 33:14 reads, "And he said, My presence shall go with thee, and I will give thee rest." Sometimes He speaks loud and clear, and sometimes He speaks in a still small voice. King David was known as a man after God's own heart (Acts 13:22). Jesus said in Matthew 11:29, "Take my yoke upon you, and *learn* of me," and in Philippians 3:10, Paul said, "That I may *know* him, and the power of his resurrection, and the fellowship of his sufferings, being made conformable unto his death".

It's my desire to walk worthy of the Lord as expressed in Colossians 1:10–11: "That ye might walk worthy of the Lord unto all pleasing, being fruitful in every good work, and increasing in the knowledge of God. Strengthened with all might, according to his glorious power, unto all patience and longsuffering with joyfulness."

As we read in Song of Solomon 2:10, "My beloved spake, and said unto me, rise up, my love, my fair one, and come away."

It is my prayer that this testimony of my journey will somehow encourage the reader to know that God Almighty is still on the throne and is involved in our daily lives.

All poetry contained in *Walk with God* is the work of the author, most of which is scripture based. It was written over the many years of her walk with God.

Lois J. Carter

Note that scripture quotations are taken from the King James Version of the Bible.

CHAPTER 1

❦

THE BEGINNING

There's always an entrance into the world, the beginning of a journey, a tale that is told. Such is the case with my story.

I was born in the small coal-mining community of Kayford, West Virginia. My father was a coal miner, and he passed away when I was just nine months old, leaving my mother to care for my two older brothers and me. She returned to her hometown of Hurricane, West Virginia, the rural area where she had grown up. My grandfather was still living at that time; my grandmother was deceased. My uncle was also living at the home.

My earliest memory is of washing my grandpa's feet on the back porch. Also, I remember my mother doing laundry with the old-time upright washing machine and washboard, then hanging the clothes outside to dry. She also drew water from an outside well that was close to our house.

My grandpa passed away shortly after that. I recall his casket being in the hallway of the house and my aunt coming to see him. She wore a long fur coat. I had never seen anything so beautiful. She had a bottle of liquor hidden up her sleeve, and of course it fell out and hit the floor. I guess she felt that the contents would help her through the ordeal at the time.

I started school at the age of five, attending a little country school not far from where we lived, which I would attend until the sixth grade. I played in the schoolyard and also played "cowboys and Indians" in our big front yard and along the creek bank. I recall running through the cornfield and also playing with our family pet, a big white cat named Snowball.

My two brothers, along with a cousin, were introduced to Pentecost through acquaintances. They were soon baptized in the name of Jesus and received the Holy Ghost with the evidence of speaking in other tongues as displayed in the book of Acts, chapter two. They became very close to Pastor E. C. Sowards Sr. of the Hurricane Apostolic Church. He always treated them like his own sons. My mother and I also began attending church, and God brought us in as well. O the power of the gospel; it is far-reaching and is alive and well today! As Acts 2:39 reads, "For the promise is unto you, and to your children, and to all that are afar off, even as many as the Lord our God shall call." This is the "living water" described in the following scriptures.

"Jesus answered and said unto her, Whosoever drinketh of this water shall thirst again. But whosoever drinketh of the water that I shall give him shall never thirst, but the water that I shall give him shall be in him a well of water springing up into everlasting life."

—John 4:13-14

"He that believeth on me, as the scripture hath said, out of his belly shall flow rivers of *living water.* (But this spake he of the Spirit, which they that believe on him should receive; for the Holy Ghost was not yet given; because that Jesus was not yet glorified.)"

—John 7:38–39

"And they were all filled with the Holy Ghost, and began to speak with other tongues as the Spirit gave them utterance".

—Acts 2:4

"And he said unto me, it is done, I am Alpha and Omega, the beginning and the end. I will give unto him that is *athirst of the fountain of the water of life freely*".

—Revelation 21:6

There Is a Fountain
There is a fountain that flows from on high
It will quench the thirst, and it will satisfy.
'Tis the living water our Lord has supplied
Given in His name since He was glorified.
So turn on the waterspout; let His Spirit flow
Down from the threshold to each soul below.
Let the deep waters now cover our souls
Let His life-giving grace heal us and make us whole.
Come ye who thirst, and drink from the waters that never run dry
O let us drink from the fountain that flows from on high.

"For these are not drunken, as ye suppose, seeing it is but the third hour of the day. But *this is that* which was spoken by the prophet Joel. And it shall come to pass in the last days, saith God, I will pour out of my Spirit upon all flesh; and your sons and your daughters shall prophesy, and your young men shall see visions, and your old men shall dream dreams".

Acts 2:15–17

This Is That
It began on the Day of Pentecost as the Spirit did descend
It blew into the upper room like a mighty, rushing wind.
At the house of Cornelius again the Spirit came
And those who received it were baptized in Jesus's name.
Many today believe His Word as the Spirit falls again
For He promised in the last days to pour it out on all men.
Although there are those who say it is not real
It is the promise of the Father; our soul it will seal.
This experience is for you no matter where you're at
Then you too can say, "My friend, *this is that!*"

Fortunately, the church bus came out to our country road and picked up those who wanted to go to church. This was a blessing since we had no transportation of our own. At least we got to attend church on the weekends. *Thank God for outreach!* We had relatives living close to us who believed in the Holy Ghost but did not baptize in the name of Jesus. There were times when we would walk to their church just to be *in* church, all the while knowing and holding to God's Word, which says there is but one God, and his name is Jesus. There were also some people who lived not too far from us who attended our church occasionally. I remember walking to their house to see if we could ride with them. If they were not planning to go, I would cry all the way back home; I wanted to go to church that much. I'm so glad that God sees the hungry heart. We still held on to God and went to church whenever we could.

Memory Verses
Memory verses, memory verses
Line upon line
With golden threads they're woven
Along my path they intertwine.
The scriptures I learned
When I was very small
Helped to mold me and shape me
So I could grow so tall.
I remember that big black Book
As I sat at Mother's knee
Verse after verse
She imparted God's Word to me.
"You must hide His Word in your heart,"
She said with a smile
"As you journey down life's pathway
It will guide your every mile.
Teach the scriptures to your children
And their children too
Forever it shall remain
A living heritage to you."

I remember those lively, powerful services. The Lord was surely present in that little country church. One night in particular, before church started, the back door of the church opened, and E. C. Sowards Jr. came dancing down the aisle in the Holy Ghost. I enjoyed the wonderful music and singing. It was anointed, and it spoke to the individual. It is a heritage that makes Pentecost unique and separate from the world. Sometimes we didn't get home until very late, but I didn't mind that at all.

My entire family was musically inclined. I used to listen to my mother play the piano and sing and worship God in our front room. We called it the parlor. My brothers could make both the piano and the guitar talk. I decided that I would try as well. Even though my feet would not reach the pedals of that big upright piano, I was determined to learn. After all, if they could do it, so could I. My brothers eventually left home to find work and marry, and I had the whole front room to myself. Music has since been a real source of enjoyment in my life. God has blessed me richly.

I am very thankful for the gospel, the death, burial, and resurrection of our Lord Jesus Christ. I am blessed to know who Jesus is. There are so many who do not know. What a joy to walk with God.

The Bible says the following things:

- That God is a spirit (John 4:24).
- That no one has seen God at any time (1 John 4:12).
- That he is omniscient, filling all time and space (Psalm 139:7–10; Jeremiah 23:24).
- That he is omnipotent (Revelation 19:6).
- That he is one ("Hear, O Israel: the Lord our God is one Lord" [Deuteronomy 6:4]).
- That he is the express image of his person (Hebrews 1:3).
- That he is the Lord, and there is none beside him (Isaiah 43:10–11).
- That he will not give his glory to another (Isaiah 42:8).
- That he is the first and the last - beside him, there is no other God (Isaiah 44:6–8).
- That whoever has seen him has seen the Father (John 14:7–10).
- That in him dwelleth all the fullness of the Godhead (Colossians 2:9).
- That he was manifest in the flesh (1 Timothy 3:16).
- That "In the beginning was the Word, the Word was with God and the Word was God. All things were made by him, and the Word was made flesh and dwelt among us" (John 1:1–14).
- That he is "Alpha and Omega, the beginning and the ending … the Almighty" (Revelation 1:8).

So, the Bible says that there is but *one* God. Isaiah 11:1-2 says, "And there shall come forth a rod out of the stem of Jesse, and a Branch shall grow out of his roots: And the spirit of the Lord shall rest upon him, the spirit of wisdom and understanding, the spirit of counsel and might, the spirit of knowledge and of the fear of the Lord." These are attributes of the one true God who created Heaven and earth, and made man after this likeness. (Reference Genesis 1:26-27 and Proverbs 8) "So God created man in his own image." Hebrews 6:13 says, "For when God made a promise to Abraham, because he could swear by no greater, *he sware by himself*." He is the same God who came to earth in the form of man to die for our sins.

Under the law, it took the yearly sacrifice of a lamb to atone for sin, always pointing to Calvary and the perfect, sinless sacrifice. Hebrews 9:22 says, "And almost all things are by the law purged with blood; and without shedding of blood is no remission." Hebrews 10:4–5 states, "For it is not possible that the blood of bulls and goats should take away sins. Wherefore when he cometh into the world he saith, sacrifice and offering thou wouldest not, but a body hast thou prepared me." So, Jesus was that lamb, the Lamb slain from the foundation of the world (Revelation 13:8).

Jesus spoke to Nicodemus in John 3:5, saying, "Verily, verily, I say unto thee, except a man be born of water and of the spirit, he cannot enter into the kingdom of God."

Jesus gave to Peter the keys to the kingdom, which Peter used when he preached on the Day of Pentecost. There were 120 people, including the Apostles and the mother of Jesus, present on that day. They all received the promise of the Holy Ghost. Acts 2:4 says "And they were all filled with the Holy Ghost and began to speak with other tongues as the Spirit gave them utterance." Acts 2:38–39 reads, "Then Peter said unto them, repent and be baptized every one of you in the name of Jesus Christ for the remission of sins, and ye shall receive the gift of the Holy Ghost. For the promise is unto you, and to your children, and to all that are afar off, even as many as the Lord our God shall call." Acts 2:41 states, "Then they that gladly received his word were baptized and the same day there were added unto them about 3000 souls." Acts 3:19 states, "Repent ye therefore, and be converted, that your sins may be blotted out, when the times of *refreshing* shall come from the presence of the Lord." *Refreshing* is defined in Isaiah 28:11–12, which reads, "For with stammering lips and another tongue will he speak to this people. To whom he said, this is the rest wherewith ye may cause the weary to rest; and this is the *refreshing*: yet they would not hear." This was the birth of the New Testament Church. I can truly say that this experience is as real today as it was on the Day of Pentecost.

Oasis of the Heart

O come, weary traveler

Stop and rest awhile

It's time to refresh

Before you go another mile.

There's an oasis in the desert

Come and drink your fill

It's free to one and all

For whosoever will.

It will always be there

For those passing by

Giving strength for the journey

To someone parched and dry.

'Tis the living water

Springing from an endless well.

For God has prepared an oasis

Wherein the heart can dwell!

Additional chapters in Acts (8:16–17, 10:44–48, and 19:5–6) show how others received the Holy Ghost and were also baptized in the name of the Lord Jesus. Thus, we fulfill the commandment in Matthew 28:19 by baptizing in the *"name"*.

"For there is none other name under heaven given among men, whereby we must be saved".

—Acts 4:12

"And Whatsoever you do in word or deed, do all in the name of the Lord Jesus".

—Colossians 3:17

"I am come in my Father's name".

—John 5:43

Jesus was the mighty God in the flesh (Emmanuel—"God with us"). He was our Father in creation, the Son in redemption, and the Holy Ghost in regeneration—one spirit.

Thank You, Jesus, for shining Your light on me.

In those early years, I rode the school bus each day. It was during these school bus rides that my opponent, a big rooster—we'll just call him Goliath—would come against me. He did not like me and always waited for me each day when I got off the bus. He had the biggest spurs I had ever seen. He would actually run toward the road to meet me when he saw the bus coming from a distance. One day I split his comb with a big switch I had hidden beside the road. He spun around and ran off. I had always dreaded to cross the footbridge, knowing he would be waiting for me. Needless to say, he wasn't too anxious to confront me after that.

Goliath

It was in my childhood, a long, long time ago
There was a situation about which you should know.
While I was living in the country among family, friends, and all
There was a certain rooster who grew to be so tall.
One day while riding the school bus, as we came around the bend
I wished with all my heart I could disappear with the wind.
I read in the Bible that Goliath was dead
But it wasn't so; he was waiting just ahead.
I saw that white streak racing to meet the bus
Goliath with his read helmet was always making a fuss.
He did not like me and longed to show how much
While I dreamed of holding him in such a "loving" clutch.
I crossed the bridge with my switch in hand
Ready to do battle as I took my stand.
With one heavy blow, his comb split down the middle
And all of a sudden that ol' rooster became very little.
He quickly spun around, staggering as off he went
I had won the battle; there was no lament.
We all face our own Goliath as our faith is surely tried
But our weapons are mighty, for God is on our side.

It was also during this time that my uncle had a nice garden, which he planted and tended each year. We also raised chickens, so we always had fresh eggs and vegetables. My mother canned lots of things and made jams and jellies to help us get through the winter. I always looked forward to Sundays, when we would have meat for dinner, usually chicken. It was very good, although I hated to see my mother wring the chicken's neck. Ouch! My uncle also raised strawberries and would pay me and some others in the area a nickel a basket to pick them. Boy, did I think I was rich! He carried the baskets of strawberries on his back several miles to town to sell them since we had no transportation of our own. We were fortunate enough to have a neighbor with a car, and once a week or so, my mother and I would ride to town with her to buy a few groceries. My treat was always an ice-cream cone from the drugstore for a whopping 10¢. I worked in the high school cafeteria during the lunch hour to receive a free lunch. Faithful God!

My mother had a friend who discovered I needed a winter coat. She asked her church for donations to purchase one for me. It was a beautiful red coat. God always meets the need.

It was also during these years that I first discovered my ability to write. My first poem was "My Daily Prayer." I did not realize at the time just how much writing would encourage me throughout my life.

My Daily Prayer

Help me, O Lord, as I begin each day
Walk with me as I travel this way.
Help me to fight and stand the test
Let me always try to do my best.
Help me to pray and not to sleep
Then, O what treasures my prayers will reap.
Help me, O Lord, to live the life
Help me to conquer envy and strife.
Help me, O Lord, this very day
Help me, O Lord. This prayer I pray.

I'm very grateful for God's blessings. He has always provided and made a way.

At the age of eleven I was stricken with polio. There were two doctors in town at that time, and fortunately they both made house calls. The doctor who came to see me told my mother that it could be the flu, but he felt it was polio. He said I needed to go to the hospital for crippled children that was located in the next town. I remember my mother crying as she stood by my bedside. We had a kind neighbor at the time, and my mother asked him if he would take me in his car to the hospital. He volunteered to call the ambulance and pay for it himself.

Once I was there, the diagnosis was confirmed by a spinal tap. I was completely paralyzed and could not lift my head from the pillow or feed myself, but we trusted in the God we serve, who gave us hope.

As I look back, I recall what I went through and how I felt at the time. I see how good God has been to me. I remember seeing some who were in "iron lungs", and one girl in particular who had had both legs removed above the knees. She was walking with artificial limbs using crutches, practicing on a walkway in front of a mirror, with help of course.

Our Pastor at the time, Reverend E. C. Sowards Sr., often came to visit me and pray for me. Special prayers were also going up at conferences and at our home church. Reverend Sowards, being a man of great insight, felt impressed of God that I would be made whole. He told my mother at church that God had impressed him that I would be coming home. We claimed, "Is any sick among you: let him call for the elders of the church; and let them pray over him, anointing him with oil in the name of the Lord. And the prayer of faith shall save the sick and the Lord shall raise him up" (James 5:14–15). I was home within three months, at which time I resumed regular school, having attended some classes while in the hospital.

Praise God! He raised me up. I am a living testimony of God's healing power. I believe God had a purpose and a plan for my life. *To God be the glory!*

The foundation was laid.

Featured in the photograph, I am in the first row on the far left. This was taken right before I was discharged from the hospital. You can see that God had brought me from total paralysis to having only weakness in my upper limbs.

In the hospital with polio

CHAPTER 2

A FAITHFUL AND FORGIVING GOD

After graduating from high school, my cousin and I traveled to Charleston, West Virginia, to take a civil service examination to be placed on a register for work with the state. God was with us, and we both did well.

A few months later, I received a call for an interview with one of the state agencies located in Huntington, West Virginia. Although it was just for a temporary three-month position at the time, I was hired and later made permanent. Once again, God had proven Himself to be faithful. My mother borrowed enough money from our neighbor for me to rent a room until I received my first paycheck. I made sure the neighbor was repaid, and always sent home as much money as I could afford to help my mother. *Thank God* that a door had swung open for me. Thus began my career with the State of West Virginia. The job would be my mainstay until retirement.

I eventually grew cold in the Lord and married outside the church. Still, my heart's desire was to serve the Lord, and I returned to my first love. Although my husband was a good man, he did not embrace my love for the church, and I walked alone for many years. Still, through it all, God was faithful. After the loss of a child through toxemia, we were delighted when a beautiful baby girl came into our lives. She is still a blessing to this day.

The Eloquent Tree
There was once a little girl who tried to climb a tree
Wondering in her heart just what she could be.
But it was quite a distance from here to way up there
Just the thought of it gave her quite a scare.
The little girl was awkward, inept to say the least
Still, she aspired to lofty heights; her determination only increased.
I can't help but wonder, were You there when I had my fall?
From the distant tree so eloquent, a graceful fall as I recall.
What it seemed was not as sought from the eloquent tree
For the dreamer of satin and lace turned out to be just plain ol' me.

The Potter

The Potter did a work
Upon the wheel of time
There, as I beheld
It seemed the clay was mine.
The hand of the Potter
Gently formed the clay
But it hardened in His hand
It was then I heard Him say,
"This vessel I must break.
But the pieces I won't lose
I will fashion once again
A vessel I can use."
So I watched the Potter
And I could clearly see
The vessel was a life
It belonged to Him, not me.
Daily He refined it
Designing His craft as such
'Til it became something beautiful
Created by the Master's touch.

I'm reminded so often of the scripture in Lamentations 3:22–23: "It is of the Lord's mercies that we are not consumed, because his compassions fail not. They are new every morning: great is thy faithfulness."

Let us examine the institution of marriage according to what the Bible says. God has always had a plan.

Marriage is defined as a union or marrying by legal ceremony of a man and woman to live together as husband and wife.

"Marriage is honorable in all, and the bed undefiled; but whoremongers and adulterers God will judge".

—Hebrews 13:4

"Have ye not read, that he which made them at the beginning made them male and female. And said, for this cause shall a man leave father and mother, and shall cleave to his wife and they twain shall be one flesh. Wherefore they are no more twain, but one flesh. What therefore God hath joined together, let no man put asunder".

—Matthew 19:4–6

"Whosoever findeth a wife findeth a good thing and obtaineth favour of the Lord".

—Proverbs 18:22

It is important that you marry in the church. To do otherwise will cause division in your home.

"Be ye not unequally yoked together with unbelievers".

—2 Corinthians 6:14

"A house divided against a house falleth".

—Luke 11:17

"Can two walk together except they be agreed"?

—Amos 3:3

Sometimes there are certain circumstances to be addressed with the believing and unbelieving spouse. These are defined in 1 Corinthians 7:10-16.

God has ordained marriage. From the beginning it was so with Adam and Eve.

Wedding Tribute
Ribbons of silk, colors so bold
Together they bind, forever to hold.
A union of two, intertwined with love
Sprinkled with blessings from the Father above.
Love tried by fire God does refine
Now as pure gold, becoming heaven's design.
Freely you give, freely you inspire
You complete me; you fulfill my desire.
Let us now affirm that we shall, we will
As long as we live. Love will be there still.
Cling to promises never to be broken
And encouraging words yet to be spoken.
Lord, give us wisdom and strength in each trial
Guide our footsteps as we travel each mile.
Flame of hope, shine brightly; dreams do come true
My love, my true love, I will always honor you.

CHAPTER 3

❧

THE FLY ON THE WALL

The next few years were challenging, but God was still leading me and encouraging me through songs and poems. I always felt that as each writing came, He was speaking to me. It lifted me up just to think He cared that much for me.

With a Song in My Heart
With a song in my heart, I have learned to face each day
When the sun is shining bright or the skies have turned to gray.
Fair is the morning with the dew upon the ground
Where love and mercy meet and grace can still be found.
God gives strength to the weary, and light when the way grows dim
For He never changes; there is no shadow of turning in Him.
I can find strength to quench life's fiery dart
As I begin each day with a song in my heart.

The enemy, however, was not ready to give up. Satan's imps are always watching for any opportunity to attack no matter what the situation, to steal what God has given His children. John 10:10 states, "The thief cometh not, but for to steal, and to kill, and to destroy: I am come that they might have life, and that they might have it more abundantly." I am reminded of Isaiah 54:17, which says, "No weapon that is formed against thee shall prosper, and every tongue that shall rise against thee in judgment thou shalt condemn. This is the heritage of the servants of the Lord, and their righteousness is of me, saith the Lord." Also, Luke 10:19 says, "Behold, I give unto you power to tread on serpents and scorpions, and over all the power of the enemy, and nothing shall by any means hurt you."

Stay the Tide
When the cares of life threaten you like a mighty rushing tide
Remember, there is one who's always on your side.
He will stay the tide
The enemy may come against you sometimes like a flood
Fear not, my child, you are covered with His blood.
He will stay the tide
When life's sea becomes tempestuous, tossing you at its will
He needs only to whisper, "Peace, be still."
He will stay the tide

"When the enemy shall come in like a flood, the Spirit of the Lord shall lift up a standard against him" (Isaiah 59:19).

Shh! Someone Is Listening!

Picture a listening device like a bug in your room or a tap on your phone. Better still, how about a fly on the wall with its antennae raised high? You try to swat it, and somehow it manages to fly away just in time, moving to another spot close by. It doesn't want to miss anything. It's annoying, nasty, and persistent. Sounds like you-know-who.

It has been advised many times over not to give Satan any praise or credit, but I also know that we must be able to recognize the enemy and be aware of his tactics before we can begin to fight him. Remember your toolbox. Ephesians 6:11–18 speaks of putting on the whole armor of God, having your loins girt with truth, having on the breastplate of righteousness, and your feet shod with the preparation of the gospel of peace, also taking the shield of faith, the helmet of salvation, the sword of the Spirit, and prayer. "For the weapons of our warfare are not carnal, but mighty through God to the pulling down of strong holds" (2 Corinthians 10:4).

Never speak negatively; always speak positively. "Death and life are in the power of the tongue: and they that love it shall eat the fruit thereof" (Proverbs 18:21). I have learned to speak faith while praising God. He is truly worthy of our praise. Psalm 34:1 says, "I will bless the Lord at all times: his praise shall continually be in my mouth."

Life's Garden

I have a garden given to me for care
And I must decide just what will grow there.
I can leave it alone to become empty and bare
Never giving it a thought. Then will come the tare.
Instead I will sow praise to keep it alive
I will sow mercy; I know it will survive.
I will sow friendship; it should grow high
So it will be seen by all those passing by.
Next the seed of faith, never the seed of doubt
For doubt will hinder growth, whereas faith will reach out.
Then the flowers will bloom with a delightful sweet smell
So that all will know my garden is doing well.
For life is a garden. Nourish it with dew from above
And it will always flourish if kept by our Savior's love.

Sometimes the roar of a lion, or the growl of a bear, makes our troubles seem larger than we are. However, the Bible says in Nahum 1:7, "The Lord is good, a strong hold in the day of trouble; and he knoweth them that trust in him." Second Timothy 1:7 says, "For God hath not given us the spirit of fear; but of power, and of love, and of a sound mind." We must hold to these promises, knowing that God will see us through.

Eye of the Storm

Today I can see the storm clouds gathering
And in the distance I can hear the thunder roll.
The wind all around me stirs up its fury
It seems everything is out of control.
But I am headed for the eye of the storm
To a place with King Jesus for the weary and worn.
I will leave behind all my trouble
My heartache, sorrow, and struggle
For they say it is calm in the eye of the storm
And there in the stillness a new peace is born.
So press on, dear pilgrim, it seems I hear Him say
You are nearing the eye of the storm, out of harm's way.
Oh come with Me to the eye of the storm
All ye heavy laden, sad and forlorn.
There in His presence He will make us whole
For in the eye of the storm He restoreth my soul.

Let us examine some building blocks for the foundation of a home. First and foremost, the foundation of your home is to be built upon God and biblical principles. He has given us the blueprints; it's up to us to follow them. To build anything takes one step at a time.

God has promised to supply all our needs if we put Him first in our lives. Matthew 6:33 says, "Seek ye first the kingdom of God and his righteousness, and all these things shall be added unto you." Joshua 24:15 states, "But as for me and my house, we will serve the Lord."

The wife should create a good, wholesome atmosphere for the family, giving full devotion to the husband and children. First Timothy 5:14 says, "I will therefore that the younger women marry; bear children, guide the house, give none occasion to the adversary to speak reproachfully." The Bible also states, "Every wise woman buildeth her house" (Proverbs 14:1). There must be boundaries in place for the well-being of the family. You cannot control others, but you can control yourself. It's up to each family member to do his or her part. It's a matter of choice.

Titus 2:1–10 serves as good instruction for both men and women as it pertains to the family. The key elements found after "The Wedding Bears" are discussed in this passage and are also justified with additional scriptures.

The Wedding Bears

I am a symbol of strength, enduring love so kind
Gentleness and forbearance in me you will find.
As you come together to be fitly joined as one
These things you should remember when each day is done.
Through patience and understanding you will learn to share
Attention to the heart brings willingness to "bear".
Bear with one another.

Sober (Mindedness)

We are to be sober-minded, solemn, serious, and sincere, focused on what's important. We are to be watchful, keenly aware, guarding, and protecting (James Strong and W. E. Vine). We should be sober both naturally and spiritually.

"Go to the ant, thou sluggard; consider her ways, and be wise."

—Proverbs 6:6

"How long wilt thou sleep, oh sluggard? When wilt thou arise out of thy sleep"?

—Proverbs 6:9

"Be sober, be vigilant, because your adversary the devil, as a roaring lion, walketh about, seeking whom he may devour".

—1 Peter 5:8

"And this know: that if the good man of the house had known what hour the thief would come, he would have watched, and not have suffered his house to be broken through".

—Luke 12:39

We must always be watchful for ourselves and for the family as a whole. The devil hates each of us because we belong to God. The devil wants to destroy us all, especially the family unit. Always be mindful of the little trouble spots.

As we read in Song of Solomon 2:15, "Take us the foxes, the little foxes, that spoil the vines, for our vines have tender grapes."

Let us pray daily for the protecting hand of God upon each member of our families.

Love for One's Husband

The wife should be dedicated, devoted, and committed. Love can only be known by the actions it produces. You've heard it said that "actions speak louder than words". Love can be expressed in many ways.

"Charity suffereth long, and is kind, charity envieth not, charity vaunteth not itself, is not puffed up" (1 Corinthians 13:4). Love should be unconditional and enduring.

Remain sweethearts. Keep the romance or true affection alive between you and your husband. "Let the husband render unto the wife due benevolence: and likewise also the wife unto the husband" (1 Corinthians 7:3).

As Christians, we should possess the fruit of the Spirit. It will help us in our daily lives as we deal not only with one another but also with those outside the home.

> "But the fruit of the Spirit is love, joy, peace, longsuffering, gentleness, goodness, faith, Meekness, temperance, against such there is no law. And they that are Christ's have crucified the flesh with the affections and lusts. If we live in the Spirit, let us also walk in the Spirit. Let us not be desirous of vain glory, provoking one another, envying one another".
>
> —Galatians 5:22–26

> "Be ye therefore followers of God, as dear children; And walk in love, as Christ also hath loved us, and hath given himself for us an offering and a sacrifice to God for a sweet smelling savour".
>
> —Ephesians 5:1–2

Love for One's Children

> "Lo, children are an heritage of the Lord: and the fruit of the womb is his reward".
> —Psalm 127:3

We should love our children and correct them.

> "He that spareth his rod hateth his son: but he that loveth him chasteneth him betimes".
> —Proverbs 13:24

> "Chasten thy son while there is hope; and let not thy soul spare for his crying".
> —Proverbs 19:18

We should also teach our children and train them in the ways of the Lord.

> "Train up a child in the way he should go: and when he is old, he will not depart from it".
> —Proverbs 22:6

We must teach our children the Bible and impress upon them the importance of regular church attendance. As they grow into teens, we should teach them to date within the church.

We should take time for our children. Listen to them, and keep communication open with them. Plan family activities as well as participation in church functions. This will help our children to grow and develop in a wholesome atmosphere. Remember, there are different stages of children's growth. If we don't teach them and lead by example, the world will do it for us.

Love will help us communicate with our family even when there are disagreements or problems. With God's help, love will help us resolve any situation if both parties choose to work toward that end. It has been said that love conquers all.

Be Discreet

Discreet means to be self-controlled, meek, tactful, careful of appearance, modest, private. Out of respect for and devotion to your family, do not speak of those things that would bring reproach or cause others to speak wrongfully of you. Let your decisions or answers be sensible and let them show your understanding.

> "He that troubleth his own house shall inherit the wind".
> —Proverbs 11:29

Be careful of your appearance.

> "In like manner also, that women adorn themselves in modest apparel, with shamefacedness and sobriety; not with broided hair, or gold, or pearls, or costly array; But (which becometh women professing godliness) with good works".
> —1 Timothy 2:9–10

"But let it be the hidden man of the heart, in that which is not corruptible, even the ornament of a meek and quiet spirit, which is in the sight of God of great price".

—1 Peter 3:4

We need to guard our hearts.

"Keep thy heart with all diligence; for out of it are the issues of life".

—Proverbs 4:23

Be Chaste

This means keeping ourselves morally pure, modest, careful of our appearance. First Peter 3:1–2 speaks of subjection in marriage and says that if any obey not the Word, they may be won by your *chaste* conversation coupled with fear.

"Flee also youthful lusts: but follow righteousness, faith, charity, peace, with them that call on the Lord out of a pure heart".

—2 Timothy 2:22

For any marriage to work, there has to be an understanding regarding faithfulness. If a relationship is to be established, the two parties are required to be faithful and devoted to each other.

When two people are married, they have already developed trust for each other to a degree, but as they grow together, they learn to depend on each other, having even more faith or confidence. Trust is earned.

There should be no unfaithfulness in the marriage.

Keep the Home Well

The wife should maintain the house, take the necessary steps to guide the family and keep order in the daily function of the household, and establish a routine. If a wife can stay at home, this is good. However, in this day and time, both husband and wife usually have to work. It takes teamwork to keep things running. Everyone, including children, must pitch in. Develop a schedule for each responsibility, and work together to accomplish it.

"In the house of the righteous is much treasure: but in the revenues of the wicked is trouble".

—Proverbs 15:6

Make your home God-centered. This should include prayer, saying grace at the table, and reading the Bible with your family. Daily bread is necessary for survival. In other words, lead by example.

Goodness

A wife should have desirable or favorable qualities or characteristics. She should be morally excellent, virtuous or upright, well-behaved, proper, and honest.

> "A virtuous woman is a crown to her husband".
>
> —Proverbs 12:4

Proverbs 31:10–31 speaks of the price of a virtuous woman, saying it is far above that of rubies. A virtuous woman cares for her family; she helps the poor and needy and speaks wisdom.

Obedience to One's Husband

The wife should be willing to do that which is required, recognizing the position of her husband (if it is the right thing). For example, if your husband gets mad and tells you to jump off a bridge or some other ridiculous thing, you know better. In other words, follow him as he follows the Lord.

> "But I would have you know that the head of every man is Christ, and the head of the woman is the man, and the head of Christ is God".
>
> —1 Corinthians 11:3

Ephesians 5:22–25 speaks of wives submitting themselves unto their own husbands as unto the Lord, while 1 Peter 3:1–7 speaks of submission, discussing how Sara obeyed Abraham.

In addition to the instructions and key components provided in Titus 2, there are many other valuable biblical nuggets to keep in mind.

Being Slow to Anger

It is important to discuss anger and forgiveness, evaluating the role they play in our lives.

> "A soft answer turneth away wrath; but grievous words stir up anger".
>
> —Proverbs 15:1

Additional verses that pertain to this subject that are not mentioned include Proverbs 15:18–28, about being slow to anger. Also, Ephesians 4:31 says, "Let all bitterness, and wrath, and anger, and clamour, and evil speaking, be put away from you, with all malice."

To be angry is to be human, but we must learn to be careful with how we answer or deal with trouble or situations that may arise in the home or elsewhere. We need to try to resolve any disagreement. As it says in Colossians 4:6, "Let your speech be always with grace, seasoned with salt."

"Be ye angry and sin not: and let not the sun go down upon your wrath: Neither give place to the devil".

—Ephesians 4:26–27

Promote Joy and Happiness

"Happy is he that hath the God of Jacob for his help, whose hope is in the Lord his God".

—Psalm 146:5

"He that handleth a matter wisely shall find good: and whoso trusteth in the Lord, happy is he".

—Proverbs 16:20

"For the joy of the Lord is your strength".

—Nehemiah 8:10

Wisdom

We need to seek wisdom in all aspects of our lives. God gives us the skill to apply good judgment to all situations.

"Happy is the man that findeth wisdom, and the man that getteth understanding".
—Proverbs 3:13

"If any of you lack wisdom, let him ask of God that giveth to all man liberally, and upbraideth not; and it shall be given him".

—James 1:5

"For wisdom is better than rubies; and all the things that may be desired are not to be compared to it".

—Proverbs 8:11

Never tell lies; always be honest.

"Lying lips are abomination to the Lord; but they that deal truly are his delight".

—Proverbs 12:22

The Apostle Paul says in Ephesians 4:25, 29: "Wherefore putting away lying, speak every man truth with his neighbor, for we are members one of another. Let no corrupt communication proceed out of your mouth, but that which is good to the use of edifying that it may minister grace unto the hearers."

Let us be forgiving and kindhearted. We should strive to be more like Jesus.

"Blessed are the merciful for they shall obtain mercy".

—Matthew 5:7

"Who is a God like unto thee, that pardoneth iniquity, and passeth by the transgression of the remnant of his heritage? he retaineth not his anger for ever, because he delighteth in mercy".

—Micah 7:18

"And forgive us our debts, as we forgive our debtors".

—Matthew 6:12

"And be ye kind one to another, tenderhearted, forgiving one another, even as God for Christ's sake hath forgiven you".

—Ephesians 4:32

Let us work hard to provide for our family.

The Apostle Paul says in Second Timothy 5:8, "But if any provide not for his own, and specially for those of his own house, he hath denied the faith, and is worse than an infidel."

"And whatsoever ye do, do it heartily, as to the Lord, and not unto men".

—Colossians 3:23

Always be thankful.

"In every thing give thanks: for this is the will of God in Christ Jesus concerning you".

—1 Thessalonians 5:18

Again, build your house upon a sure foundation, one of biblical principles. There will always be problems or situations to deal with, but God is a present help to lead you and guide you. There should always be harmony and the willingness to work together to achieve any goal. The family mirrors the Lord Jesus Christ and His church. The "fly on the wall" is always present, but remember these scriptures:

"Beloved, think it not strange concerning the fiery trial which is to try you, as though some strange thing happened unto you: But rejoice, inasmuch as ye are partakers of Christ's sufferings; that, when his glory shall be revealed, ye may be glad also with exceeding joy".

—1 Peter 4:12–13

"Ye are of God, little children, and have overcome them: because greater is he that is in you, than he that is in the world".

—1 John 4:4

CHAPTER 4

THE POWER OF PRAYER

"Oh thou that hearest prayer, unto thee shall all flesh come".

—Psalm 65:2

Did You Think to Pray
When you arose this morning, did you think to pray?
Lest thou dash thy foot against a stone, or a snare be in thy way.
Our footsteps are ordered; the direction we must take.
So it's best to ask for guidance with each day we awake:
"Give us, Lord, our daily bread; make it sufficient for the day."
Your path will be much smoother; you'll be glad you thought to pray.

"Early will I seek thee"

—Psalm 63:1

"My voice shalt thou hear in the morning. Oh Lord, in the morning will I direct my prayer unto thee, and will look up".

—Psalm 5:3

"The Lord will hear when I call unto him".

—Psalm 4:3

"The Lord hath heard my supplication, the Lord will receive my prayer".

—Psalm 6:9

The Lover of My Soul

As the morning breaks, the air fresh with dew
With great anticipation my lover I pursue.
Ever so patiently, He waits to hear me say
"O lover of my soul, dine with me today."
Flee loneliness, flee all doubt and fear
For my lover now awaits, my lover oh so dear.
As shades of evening come and night begins to fall
I search for my lover; He hearkens to my call.
He is my beloved, the heartbeat of my soul
I am under his spell, lost in His control.
A tapestry of love He weaves around my heart
Each thread so carefully chosen for His greatest work of art.

Anatomy of Prayer

Enter His presence with a thankful heart, worshipping our Lord and Savior, for He is worthy of our praise. Philippians 4:6 says, "Be careful for nothing; but in everything by prayer and supplication with thanksgiving let your requests be made known unto God."

We must believe or accept that what we desire can be obtained. Hebrews 11:1 says, "Now faith is the substance of things hoped for, the evidence of things not seen." Pray with purpose and meaning, seeking His will in all things. Be specific as to what you are praying about (substance), picturing it in your mind as coming to pass (evidence) even though you cannot actually see it now. We must encourage ourselves through the word of God. Romans 10:17 says, "So then faith cometh by hearing, and hearing by the word of God."

"If thou canst believe, all things are possible to him that believeth".

—Mark 9:23

"And all things whatsoever ye shall ask in prayer, believing, ye shall receive".

—Matthew 21:22

"If ye have faith as a grain of mustard seed, ye shall say unto this mountain, remove hence to yonder place, and it shall remove, and nothing shall be impossible unto you".

—Matthew 17:20

"The effectual fervent prayer of righteous man availeth much".

—James 5:16

"Death and life are in the power of the tongue, and they that love it shall eat the fruit thereof".

—Proverbs 18:21

God has a way of getting our attention, causing us to see our need of Him. It was in 1978 when my husband suffered a heart attack. I could see the hand of God reaching for a lost soul.

The next few years brought open-heart surgery and disability. My husband began to seek the Lord. God began to deal with him in dreams also. My husband dreamed he was in a house, and a storm came up and shook the house, making him very afraid. I told him that was him: his house or temple. He had a struggle with cigarettes but knew he needed to follow his doctor's advice. I saw him put them down, never to pick them up again. He said, "Lord, if You're really real, take the desire for these from me." Our pastor visited my husband frequently in the hospital, and my husband promised he would come to church. He was true to his word and told me he wanted to get saved. Remember, Matthew 19:26 says, "But with God all things are possible." My prayers were answered when my husband was baptized and came into the church, but much to my disappointment, he grew cold in the Lord. He was still very ill with COPD and was hospitalized frequently.

It was during this period that there was a "revisit" of polio on those who were childhood victims. It was mentioned in most news broadcasts. The enemy again tried to tell me I was done for, that I would lose my job and my insurance, leaving me with no way to care for my family. Of course, Satan is the father of all liars, and God did not allow that to happen. I'm so glad our God is in charge and that He hears and answers prayer. Hebrews 4:16 states, "Let us therefore come boldly unto the throne of grace that we might obtain mercy, and find grace to help in the time of need." Psalm 50:15 tells us, "And call upon me in the day of trouble; I will deliver thee, and thou shalt glorify me."

It's Me Again, Lord
As I travel today down life's troubled road
My steps grow weary, and heavy is my load.
But He says, "Take courage. You're not alone
Just come boldly before the throne."
Sometimes I'm up; sometimes I'm down
I search for answers, but none can be found.
I just turn to Jesus; I know He'll see me through
He said, "Draw nigh to Me; I'll draw nigh to you."
And then Satan whispers, "There's no need to pray"
I'm more determined than I was yesterday.
For my every need I know You can meet
That's why I lay them all down at Your feet.
Yes, it's me again, Lord; I'm on my knees in prayer
It's me again, Lord; You said You'd meet me there.
And all my burdens, You promised You would bear
So upon You, dear Lord, I cast my every care.

It was during these years that God encouraged me even more through dreams, poems, and songs. So deep and meaningful they were to me. What a blessing! One dream I had that was very profound was the tunnel dream. I was running through a tunnel with open doors on each side. As I passed by each door, I would say, "In the name of Jesus." I could see the light at the end of the tunnel. God was showing me the end of the trial, telling me to hold on and keep going. At the next church service I attended, there was a message in tongues and interpretation in which God confirmed my dream. The last line of the interpretation said, "Then you shall see My light at the end of the tunnel, and you will shine for Me." *Wow!* I was stunned since I had not told anyone of the dream. *What a faithful God! Tongues and interpretation occurs when God moves on a Holy Ghost filled individual to speak in another language to convey a message from God. The message is then interpreted for all to understand. This may be by the same individual or by someone else as God directs. This is one of the gifts of the Spirit as described in 1 Corinthians 12, 14. It is for the edification of the church and a sign to the non-believer.* The gifts of the Spirit are very much alive and working in the church today.

Light at the End of the Tunnel

Many years I have traveled through this earth down here
Sometimes I have sorrow; sometimes I have fear.
But I hear Him say to me, "Look not to the left or right
Keep your eyes on the straight and narrow, for the end is just in sight."
I remember what He said when my nights seemed very long
"The race won't be to the swiftest, nor the battle to the strong."
So I know if I keep running in this race with all my might
Soon I'll pass from the darkness and enter the light.
For I see the light at the end of the tunnel. Straight ahead, it's in my view
It gives me strength to keep on going; all my hope it does renew.
And soon I'll reach the end; my journey will then be past
I'll praise my Lord and Savior for seeing me safely home at last!

In 1997, our pastor Reverend E. S. Harper designated the year as the Year of the Scarlet Thread and the Year to Save Our Families (a reference to Joshua 2:18). I purposed in my heart that this would be *my* year. I held to the red cord that Pastor Harper had made available to everyone as a symbol, and claimed my family. Isaiah 59:1 says, "Behold the Lord's hand is not shortened that it cannot save neither his ear heavy that it cannot hear."

Our God Is Able

Our God is able, abundantly so
To do much more than our hearts could ever know.
Blessings flow like a river from His throne on high
His storehouse is rich with a bountiful supply.
So ask in faith, believing that the answer He will send
For His promises are as a rainbow, and His love is without an end.

In November 1997, my daughter came into the church. She was baptized in the name of Jesus and was filled with the Holy Ghost. My husband also began to seek the Lord again. First Corinthians 7:14 states "For the unbelieving husband is sanctified by the wife," and verse 16 states, "For what knowest thou, O wife, whether thou shalt save thy husband?"

The God of Now

There is someone who takes good care of me
One who's always there whatever the need may be.
He's my present help with each and every task
And all I ever need to do is go to Him and ask.
For He's all sufficient, called the Great I Am
My Savior and Redeemer known as Calvary's Lamb.
He blesses me daily, though I cannot tell you why
For I am unworthy that He should love one such as I.
The past, present, and future; He's the Ancient of Days
Unto Jesus be all glory, honor, and praise.
At His feet, my heart and soul now bow
For I can truly say that He is the God of now!

My Lord continues to hear and answer prayer, providing my needs as well as the needs of my family and many others. He is truly a prayer-answering God. Our pastor recently preached a wonderful message entitled "You and God Are a Majority." I have found that to be so true. Majority rules! Romans 8:31 says, "If God be for us, who can be against us?" There were times when it seemed as if the heavens were closed and I felt like Job did in Job 23:3: "Oh that I knew where to find him! That I might come even to his seat!" God, however, was always there, for He will never leave or forsake His children. He is our rock as described in Psalm 61:1-2 which reads, "Hear my cry, O God; attend unto my prayer. From the end of the earth will I cry unto thee; when my heart is overwhelmed, lead me to the rock that is higher than I." Job 23:10 says, "But he knoweth the way that I take; when he hath tried me I shall come forth as gold." We must keep holding to His hand, knowing He will always be faithful and that He is working all things for our good.

Your Help Is Just a Prayer Away

If you have a burden you can no longer bear
If you have a heartache and you need someone to care,
Just bring it to Jesus; call on Him today
You'll find your help is just a prayer away.
For there is a storehouse with a vast supply
There is a fountain that never runs dry.
There are healings and miracles, blessings and more
Knock, for your help is just at the door.
So let not the flame of hope grow dim
Just keep on believing; keep on trusting Him.
No matter what trouble at your door may lay
Remember, your help is just a prayer away.

Prayer of Deliverance

May heaven's arms embrace you and hold you always secure
May the hand of God lead you through all you must endure.
May His eyes ever behold you with tender loving care
May you hear Him gently whisper, "Your sorrow I will share."
May you find an inner peace emanating from God above
May wings of mercy lift you as you hold to His great love.

I'm reminded of Isaiah 65:24 which states, "And it shall come to pass that before they call, I will answer; and while they are yet speaking, I will hear." Also, Jeremiah 33:3 says "Call unto me, and I will answer thee, and shew thee great and mighty things, which thou knowest not."

As James 4:8 tells us, "Draw nigh to God, and he will draw nigh to you." Remember, God is never too busy!

"But the prayer of the upright is his delight".

—Proverbs 15:8

"For the eyes of the Lord are over the righteous, and his ears are open unto their prayers".

—1 Peter 3:12

Rest with the assurance that God is faithful and will answer in His own time and according to His will. *There is power in prayer.*

CHAPTER 5

THE SHADOW OF DEATH

In 1979 I lost my mother. She suffered a stroke and was unconscious for about two weeks before passing away. She had not been well for several years. Even though it hurt to lose her, I knew my mother had lived for God for many years, so I was confident she was ready to meet the Lord.

The Shadow of Death
When death casts its shadow, our hearts ache within
But God is our comfort; His Word He doth send.
To brighten the flickering candle that it may shine through the night
'Til at last the dawn greets us, hope will ever cast its light.

In 1986 I lost my oldest brother. He also had not been well for several years. The Lord had dealt with me for months about the Twenty-Third Psalm. I did not make a connection with my brother at the time, thinking it was perhaps another poem or song. It would appear at any given time. The verses would repeat over and over in my mind and sometimes would not leave, particularly verse 4, concerning the "valley of the shadow of death".

Soon after that, I received a call that my brother had passed away. My husband and I left immediately, driving to Florida, where he lived. At the time I did not remember these verses of scripture. It was as if God had temporarily erased them from my mind. When we arrived at the funeral home, I picked up one of the memorial handouts. There on the inside was the Twenty-Third Psalm. It was as though it leaped off the page at me. God spoke to me immediately: "Now you know what I was telling you." That was a comfort, as was the fact my brother had lived for God. God again had proven to be faithful.

Our Rose of Sharon
Like the fragrance of a rose captured in its bloom
So is the love of Jesus; His presence fills the room.
Bringing hope and cheer to brighten your day
For He is our Comforter each step of life's way.
Through each valley, may you find Him always near
Just speak His name; He will calm your every fear.

A short while after I returned home, the Lord gave me a dream. In the dream I was driving down a road and passed by my mother, who was walking along. Naturally, I stopped to pick her up. She told me, "No, you go on. James [my brother] is here now, and it's all right." God was telling me to travel on. It's always encouraging when God speaks to me like that. It enabled me to heal and move forward. Ecclesiastes 3:4 states, "A time to weep, and a time to laugh, a time to mourn, and a time to dance." God knows we need that to heal. If we have the Spirit of God, He will comfort us, strengthen us, and give us peace.

Over the years, my husband had grown progressively worse. In 1997, he passed away, ending his many years of suffering. Death had visited us again.

Grieving
At this time of grieving, may you find the Savior near
For He is acquainted with your sorrow. Therefore, friend, you need not fear.
He will be with you, your heavy load to bear
A present help in the time of trouble, our Lord will always be there.

While I was completing this particular chapter, my last living sibling passed away. He too had been ill for quite some time. I rest with the assurance that he too made his peace with God and has joined the family gone before. I had been so burdened, weeping and praying for a week prior to this. While on his death bed, my brother began to call the names of those gone on to Heaven (our mother and older brother). The Holy Ghost began to witness through my brother as he prayed for God to take him home. Thank God his suffering has ended. What a reunion day we will have!

"For we know that if our earthly house of this tabernacle were dissolved, we have a building of God, an house not made with hands, eternal in the heavens. For in this we groan, earnestly desiring to be clothed upon with our house which is from heaven".
—2 Corinthians 5:1–2

"Naked came I out of my mother's womb, and naked shall I return thither: the Lord gave, and the Lord hath taken away; blessed be the name of the Lord".
—Job 1:21

A few months after my brother's passing, I began to have a problem with what I thought was indigestion, which would come and go. One day in particular, I was in the grocery store and began to feel bad again. I felt impressed to go to the ER. While I was there, tests revealed that my cardiac enzymes were elevated and that one side of my heart was not functioning as strongly as it should. The enzymes went down after a while, and the doctor was going to send me home. However, a cardiologist felt I had blockages and wanted to do a heart catheterization, which did confirm that I had blockages. That led to open-heart surgery. Through everything, God gave me an inner peace that it would be all right either way. I'm so glad He was not finished with me.

Soon after this, I began to have issues with my feet. My toes were very sore and dark. I decided again to go to the ER. I was referred to a rheumatologist, but my appointment was several months away. The next day, while I was eating breakfast, that voice spoke again, telling me to call right then to see if there had been a cancellation. Upon calling, I was told there had been no cancellations. However, as soon as I returned to finish breakfast, the doctor's office called. While I had been talking to them, someone was canceling their appointment on the other line. So, the doctor was able to take me that same morning. Our God is an on-time God, a present help in the time of trouble. I was able to get the treatment I needed for my poor circulation. I feel this was divine intervention.

Thank God for His faithfulness through it all. Hebrews 13:5 says, "I will never leave thee, nor forsake thee." And Matthew 28:20 says, "Lo I am with you always, even unto the end of the world."

The God of Hope

He is the God of hope, making His children glad
He lifts the heavyhearted, giving joy unto the sad.
He is our shining light to guide us all the way
Along with our hope for tomorrow and our help for today.

CHAPTER 6

❧

FOR SUCH A TIME AS THIS

(Called to Serve the Lord)

As we move forward working in his kingdom, I am reminded of Acts 1:8, "But ye shall receive power after that the Holy Ghost is come upon you, and ye shall be witnesses unto me both in Jerusalem, and in all Judaea, and in Samaria, and unto the *uttermost part of the earth.*" We are all called to be witnesses. Additional scriptures pertaining to service are listed in this chapter.

"Many be called, but few chosen".

—Matthew 20:16

"Then saith he unto his disciples. The harvest truly is plenteous, but the laborers are few: Pray ye therefore the Lord of the harvest, that he will send forth laborers into his harvest".

—Matthew 9:37–38

The Master's Field
There's a field that's now white to view
Behold, the laborers are few.
Say not four months the harvest will be
For it is ready to gather to me.
But who will work in the Master's field
Join the reapers to gather earth's yield.
Who will answer His cry
Saying, "Lord, here am I"?
Can you hear Him calling to you
"Come, there is much work to do.
Life's precious wheat is wasting away
Won't you work in My field today?"
Oh, we must work while it is light
Soon the day will turn into night.
And each tomorrow will become yesterday
As the times of the Gentiles pass away.

"Also I heard the voice of the Lord, saying, whom shall I send, and who will go for us? Then said I, Here am I; send me".

—Isaiah 6:8

Go Forth to Conquer

Go forth to conquer, be it on land or sea
Go forth to conquer; the Lord is with thee.
Wheresoever thou goest, He has promised to lead
If we will only hearken through Him, we can succeed.
Whatsoever is bound or loosed, it shall remain the same
When we unleash the power contained in Jesus's name.
Go forth to conquer; the cry is heard again
Go forth to conquer; there is victory over sin.

Go Tell My People

Go. Go tell My people; tell them I died to set them free
Tell them I will soon be coming. Make ready My children, My bride-to-be.
Go out, go out, dear servant, go quickly to the streets and lanes
Even to the hedges and highways. Bid them come, the poor and maimed.
Bid them come to my wedding supper, free to all, whosoever will
Tell them to come, for all is ready; there is room in My house to fill.
Tell them to make preparation, to be ready to enter that day
For they must wear the wedding garment. O how sad to be turned away.

"I beseech you therefore, brethren, by the mercies of God, that ye present your bodies a living sacrifice, holy, acceptable unto God, which is your reasonable service. And be not conformed to this world: but be ye transformed by the renewing of your mind, that ye may prove what is that good, and acceptable, and perfect, will of God".

—Romans 12:1–2

"Wherefore we receiving a kingdom which cannot be moved, let us have grace, whereby we may serve God acceptably with reverence and godly fear".

—Hebrews 12:28

Total Submission

I am devoted to You, Lord; I give myself to Thee
In Your service, Lord, a living sacrifice I'll be.
A vessel for the Master's use. Fulfill Your will in me
Try me, Lord, I say, for I'm Yours totally.
An ambassador in Your Kingdom, the glad news proclaim
I will advance the cause to glorify Your name.
Total submission: it's the least I can do
To show how much I care for someone as worthy as You!

"Having then gifts differing according to the grace that is given to us..."

—Romans 12:6

"A man's gift maketh room for him, and bringeth him before great men".

—Proverbs 18:16

"For the gifts and calling of God are without repentance".

—Romans 11:29

God has a plan for each one of us, and He will use us if we are willing. There was a dear old saint who used to tell us that God is not as concerned with our ability as He is with our availability. Let us also not forget to support our pastor. We must hold up his hands just as they did for Moses in the battle with the Israelites and Amalek (Exodus 17:11–12). May we ever be mindful of these things as we seek His will in our lives.

I'll Follow You

Oh God, my Father, before You I bow
To ask direction; hear me just now.
For I'm trusting in You, Lord, to show me the way
And, Lord, I will follow, Thy will obey.
There are times in my life that I know not what to do
It's then I turn to You, Lord; I know You'll see me through.
If I acknowledge You in all my ways
You'll direct my path for the rest of my days.
I'll be ready and willing, faithful and true
So wherever You lead, Lord, I'll follow You.
For Thou art the Shepherd, and I am the sheep
Through the valley I'll follow, climb the mountain steep.
And Your voice I will answer; none other will do
Yes, I have decided, I'll follow You.

Ecclesiastes 9:10 states, "Whatsoever thy hand findeth to do, do it with thy might." I have always played music in church, whenever and wherever there was a need. And, of course, I still enjoy writing. There is a place for each of us to labor in the Master's field. Our goal should always be soul winning.

Cast Your Net on the Right Side
Simon Peter was standing by the lake one day
When our dear Lord passed by that way.
The disciples had toiled all night, and no fish were caught
"Let down your net," Jesus said. "Get ready for a draught."
The voice of our Lord can still be heard today
Calling to mankind as He passes by our way.
"Come follow Me. I will make you fishers of men
For I long to free all people from sin."
So launch out into the deep, there with the Savior to abide
Just cast your net on the right side.

Esther 4:14 says, "And who knoweth whether thou are come to the kingdom for such a time as this." Esther had great courage. God helped her obtain the favor of the king to save her people.

My heart's desire has always been to be called, chosen, and used for God's glory with the gifts God has given me—an encouragement to someone, a Good Samaritan to rescue a lost soul. Jude 1:23 states, "And others save with fear, pulling them out of the fire, hating even the garment spotted by the flesh." Let us strive to be that vessel of honor for the master's use as described in Second Timothy 2:21. Finally, let us not forget these two important scriptures: First Corinthians 15:58 states, "Therefore, my beloved brethren, be ye stedfast, unmoveable, always abounding in the work of the Lord, forasmuch as ye know that your labor is not in vain in the Lord." And Second Peter 1:10 which states, "Wherefore the rather, brethren, give diligence to make your calling and election sure: for if ye do these things, ye shall never fall."

A Time Such as This

To everything there is a season
A time for every purpose or reason.
A time to be born, a time to die
A time to laugh, a time to cry.
There's a time to plant and a time to reap
A time to awake, a time to sleep.
A time of war, a time of bliss
It could be a time such as this.
There was a time to redeem the lost
It reached from Calvary to Pentecost.
When the Holy Spirit Jesus promised to send
Came as a rushing mighty wind.
Even today, just as before
His Spirit again He will pour.
So now is the time for believin'
It's the time for receivin'.
There is a time our Lord will come again
Watch for you know not when.
It could be tomorrow; it could be today
He will catch His bride away.
So seize this moment; it's yours and mine
For soon we'll be out of time.
What if His coming we should miss?
It could be a time such as this.
So could He be declaring
That we would be sharing
A time such as never before
For salvation is near, even at the door?

CHAPTER 7

THE CHRISTIAN'S CALENDAR

We have certain special days that we celebrate each month—birthdays, anniversaries, official holidays, etc.—but I feel each month should also have an appropriate Christian theme to serve as a reminder of the Christian's daily walk with the Lord.

"To everything there is a season, and a time to every purpose under the heavens".
—Ecclesiastes 3:1

Daily Calendar
Good morning, God. How are You today?
I know I should talk to You, there's so much I need to say.
But I'm really too busy now with cleaning and laundry to do
I've lots of errands to run before the day is through.
So I need to get started. The coupons first I'll clip
After my coffee is ready; let me first take a sip.
Then off I go to buy groceries and more
I always look for bargains at each and every store.
And I told Mrs. Jones I'd stop by this afternoon
I know You won't mind, God. I promise we'll talk real soon.
Next there are meals to be cooked and kids to be fed
Baths to be drawn, then homework and bed.
My! But I'm exhausted. Time to go to sleep
Whatever I had to say, God, well, I guess it will have to keep.

JANUARY

A New Year

Another year has come to an end
Its moments recorded in a timeless blend.
Resolutions once again have been made
Only to be broken and eventually fade.
So let us begin the New Year with a sacred vow
Ready to face the challenges that lie before us now.
May we ever be mindful of the present hour
As we move forward in truth and power.
There is work yet to be done
Many souls yet to be won.
There are new horizons yet to see
Greater miracles yet to be.
Let us put our hands to the plow
A church in action with a vision for now.
We resolve and agree as on Jesus we lean
By faith to reach for those things yet unseen.

FEBRUARY

To My Special Valentine
How much do I love Thee
There are no words to say.
You're sweeter than a honeycomb
Kind and gentle in every way.
I love to steal away
Just to be alone with You
Those precious quiet times
That thrill me through and through.
You're as refreshing as a waterfall
On a hot summer day
You're the light dancing through the trees
That helps me find my way.
You control the strings of my heart
Together our spirits agree
You write each note and strike each cord
To form love's musical melody.
When I think of You,
My heart skips a beat
You are my everything
You make my life complete.
So I'm sending this Valentine
Wrapped with praise that rings so true
It contains this special message:
Dear Lord, I love You!

MARCH

March Winds are Blowing

March winds are blowing
I hear the distant sound
I feel the wind brush against me
As the forces of nature abound.
But I hear a different sound
That of a rushing, mighty wind
This wind blew at Pentecost
As God's Spirit did descend.
It was a sound from Heaven
A promise made to all
That in the last days
The Holy Ghost would fall.
Born of water and spirit
To Nicodemus it was told
Peter proclaimed it in his message
As he stood that day so bold.

Let us rise to the occasion
Stir up the gift within you
Equipped to meet the challenge
In each and everything you do.
God has promised to be with us
The church known by His name
There are souls yet to be born
The process is still the same.
With spiritual fire and fervor
Proclaim it loud and clear
Let this be the desire of the church
Lord, speak to whomsoever will hear.
WINDS OF PENTECOST: BLOW ON!

APRIL

Behold the Seeds

I hold a tiny seed
In the palm of my hand
Just how it can produce
Is hard to understand.
But the contents of the seed
Have been hidden from man
The task of sowing and reaping
Is part of a bigger plan.
After the seed has been sown
There comes a time to nourish.
And with the proper watering
The seed will grow and flourish.
Let us now consider
How wonderful it is to see
That, which by faith
The seed can grow to be.
God has provided these seeds
And has told us what to do
If we follow His instructions
He has promised a harvest too.
What will we do with the seeds in our hands?

Celebrate!

Our Savior lives!
Matthew 27–28,
The crucifixion and resurrection
of our
Lord Jesus Christ.
HAPPY EASTER

MAY

A Tribute to Mother
Thank you, Mother
For teaching me to pray
And for taking me to church
That I might learn the right way.
You were my example
In word and in deed
You lived the life before me
You planted the seed.
Ofttimes I've wondered
Just how you made ends meet
But through those times of disappointment
You remained so sweet.
You knew our Heavenly Father
Would always make a way
And the God of my childhood
Is the one I trust today.

JUNE

Father

Our Heavenly Father designed
A father to lead
To be the head of the house
Providing the family's needs.
One who's strong but gentle
Desiring to succeed
Who daily prays for wisdom
God's voice he will heed!
(The family mirrors Christ and His church.)

JULY

Three Cheers for the Red, White, and Blue
Mine eyes have caught a glimpse
Of a church shining so bright
Washed in crimson red
Trimmed in purest white.
Rich and refined
Much like a sapphire blue
Tried in the fire
Standing faithful and true.
A church on the move
Marching to victory's place
A bride prepared and waiting
Adorned with God's gentle grace.
Let us wave the banner high
Fighting against all wrong
Let us rejoice and celebrate
As together we sing freedom's song.

AUGUST

Like An Eagle

Like a mighty eagle
Let my spirit soar
Carry me away
To heights I've never reached before.
On the wings of an eagle
Lord, bring strength to me
May I be ever watchful
Give me eyes to see.
Let not mine enemy
Overtake me in flight
Lord, help me to find
My way in the night.
I wait with understanding
Hope is the song I sing
Rise up, faith, rise up
Like an eagle's wing.
Cover me with Your feathers.
Hide me under Your wing
You are my shelter, Lord
To Your promises I cling.
Thou art a symbol
Strength and courage You bring
O great and mighty eagle
Bear me up on Your wing.

Faith

Faith is belief with action. It is the substance of things hoped for, the evidence of things not seen (Hebrews 11:1).

To each of us is given a measure of faith (Romans 12:3), yet sometimes in life our faith is weak. We become discouraged and find it difficult to reach out. That's when God's Word will strengthen and encourage our hearts (Romans 10:17). The Holy Ghost will intercede in our lives when we pray and believe (Jude 1:20). For without faith it is impossible to please Him (Hebrews 11:6). It is written, the just shall live by faith (Romans 1:17).

We truly serve a prayer-answering God. For with God, all things are possible (Matthew 19:26).

SEPTEMBER

HEADLINE NEWS
The Harvest Is Ripe
★★WORKERS NEEDED★★

Workers are needed
The field now awaits
The harvest indeed is ripe
Please report at the gates.
We are God's hands
He's depending on us to do
He will give us strength
For the laborers are few.
Many have toiled
And planted the seed
Others have plowed and watered
Recognizing the need.
What a privilege to serve
To seek no applause
Let us not forget
This just and worthy cause.
We cannot allow
Life's harvest to waste away
It belongs to the Master
His will we must obey.
May God send the willing
While there is light
The fruit is ripe for picking
The field is already white.

OCTOBER

Beauty in Darkness

There is beauty in darkness. As we celebrate the change of season with its beautiful colors and fall parties, the church remains the true beauty shining in a dark world—the pearl of great price. It has been likened unto a treasure hidden in a field, yet the world comprehends it not.

Jesus is the true light of the world, our Savior and our guide. If we trust Him and hold to His hand, He will show us the way. All good things shall be manifested in His own time. Like a seed planted in the ground, hidden in darkness, that which is good will grow and burst forth into something beautiful. A city set on a hill cannot be hidden. It will shine through the darkness.

Let us praise our God, the Creator of all the beauty we enjoy.

NOVEMBER

A Thankful Heart

O great and mighty God
Maker of wind and rain
Who can harness Your greatness?
What is it that can contain?
All things speak of Your majesty
They tell of your fame
I call them to remembrance
As I seek to honor Your name.
Thank You, Lord, for daily care
Food, shelter, satin, and lace
Thank You for salvation
For Your amazing grace.
You mean everything to me
My strength and my fortress Thou art
May I always be grateful
Lord, give me a thankful heart.

Thanksgiving

Thanksgiving is a special day to gather with family and friends to count our blessings as we reflect upon God's goodness to us, a time to share our bounty with others.

As we partake of the "horn of plenty", let us not forget God's spiritual blessings to the church. We should offer praise to the One who hath redeemed us. Psalm 34:1 says, "I will bless the Lord at all times: his praise shall continually be in my mouth." The Holy Ghost enables us to commune with Jesus at all times. "Our Lord cares and provides for his people. He daily loadeth us with his benefits" (Psalm 68:19).

When we enter His sanctuary, we should enter with thanksgiving as we feast on His many blessings and bask in His presence. His table is always full of good things. What a privilege to dine with the Master.

DECEMBER

The Gift of Christmas

Christmas is a gift
Sent from above
It contains many blessings
Wrapped in His great love.
Jesus brought this gift
To the world below
At Bethlehem's manger
It began to grow.
So, remembering the season
And the friends we hold dear
Here's hoping your Christmas
Is filled with all goodness and cheer.
MERRY CHRISTMAS

The True Christmas Gift

To *know* Christ is to *know* Christmas, for *no* Christ means *no* Christmas.

It's so easy to get caught up in the hustle and bustle of the holidays with all the wonderful festivities, the giving and the getting, and forget what it is that we're really celebrating—the birth of Jesus (Isaiah 9:6). Let us not forget why He came (John 3:16; Romans 5:8). It was the ultimate gift of love.

The same love living within our hearts should reflect His nature as we, the church, take His message of hope to the dying world (Romans 5:5; Philippians 2:5). To truly know Him is to know Him as the Creator (deity) and our Savior (the Lamb slain from the foundation of the world). He was revealed at Bethlehem's manger as Jesus and as Christ, the Anointed One (Matthew 1:18, 21; Luke 2:11, 4:18).

We honor you, dear Lord, as we celebrate Your birth. You are indeed a wonder. *Happy birthday!*

CHAPTER 8

THE LIGHTER SIDE

Sometimes it helps to laugh at ourselves and the funny situations that we encounter in life. It helps us to find peace.

"A time to weep, and a time to laugh; a time to mourn, and a time to dance".

—Ecclesiastes 3:4

"A merry heart doeth good like a medicine, but a broken spirit drieth the bones".

—Proverbs 17:22

Attention, Mighty Warrior

Let me tell you a story. Need I say it's true?

There was a time recently when only God could see me through.

A pinched nerve I had. It seemed so unfair

So much pain and suffering: it seemed I could not bear.

Much prayer was held. God blessed me so

My back and leg got better; once again I was on the go.

A few days later, much to my surprise …

I did not see it coming. I guess I wasn't wise.

I stopped by the grocery store to buy a thing or two

Little did I know what was about to ensue.

As I approached my steps, what happened I do not know

The groceries took flight while my knees took quite a blow.

The landing was hard. I know that much for sure

O, dear Lord, how much more can I endure?

Well, I gained my presence of mind and looked to see the world and all

For I knew that God (and wondered who else) had surely seen me fall.

I stumbled in the house with two sore and bleeding knees

My leg and ankle bruised. Again, Lord, help me please.

The next few days were challenging, yet there was more to come

It was while I was at the sink; uh-oh, where did that water come from?

A water line had broken, flooding my bathroom and hall

The water then flowed downward, until the ceilings began to fall.

Of course I was in a panic, not knowing what to do

But soon it didn't matter; by then I'd lost my mind too.

When I came to myself, I found that my car needed gas

So down the road I went, but, oh my, alas!

I talked to the devil and told him he was a liar

It was then the attendant told me about the nail in my front tire.

Well, God has brought me through; I'm still in His hand

This final word I leave with you: Oh my, ain't life grand!

PS: Look in the back of the Book. *We win!*

Lois Sez

The daily menu should include a serving of the living bread.

The snail is a good example: It's willing to run the race with patience.

The flavor of the day is the spice of life. Taste the Lord and see.

Today is yesterday's tomorrow. Choose wisely.

Dress to kill. Put on the whole armor of God.

Can't see where you're going? Follow the light of the world.

Too much baggage will cause the mountain climber to be top-heavy. Lay aside all excess weight.

A thimble of hope + a teaspoon of effort = a measure of faith.

Each step forward will keep you on the "straight and narrow".

Red Alert

'Twas the night before the rapture, and on the earth below
There was noise and confusion; people were running to and fro.
I heard all the commotion. It was meaningless and loud
I decided to take a look, so I peered out over a cloud.
I couldn't believe my eyes. It was all plainly there
As the Lord stood ready, there were many unaware.
"Send one of Your servants," I said, "so the people may hear
'Time to get ready. The King of Glory will soon appear.'
As it is written, in the night there shall be light
It's sufficient for the journey. Declare ye that which is right."
I see them now repenting. They're being baptized all the same
For to be the bride, they need to wear His name.
Believe the servant's report: ye must be reborn
Born of the water and the Spirit, for He cometh in the morn.

My Pet Peeve

I carried it in my pocket when it was fast asleep
Nobody had one just like it. I felt it was mine to keep.
Sometimes I brought it out and wore it on my sleeve
For I wanted the world to see: I had my very own "pet peeve".
I feared that I would lose it. Of that I could not conceive
For we had become close friends, just me and my pet peeve.
I often embraced it, hoping it would never leave
It meant so much to me, my lovely "pet peeve"
One day it became too heavy. Others offered to relieve
But I did not want to share; after all, it was my "pet peeve".
Finally it was crushed. I was too busy to grieve
And so goes the story of me and my "pet peeve".

My Wits' End

Today I took a journey of which I now do speak
For as in my times before, my sanity I did seek.
It's been a day like many others, when everything goes wrong
It began early this morning and lasted all day long.
The ride was bumpy to say the least; I fought to stay on the road
Somehow I had to make it to that special place of abode.
Soon I'll get to where I'm going; I'll rest when I arrive
But in the meantime, Lord, just help me to survive.
My spirit is a little low, but I know, Lord, that You care
So send a little sunshine. Have it waiting for me there.
Well, at last I've reached it, the place where I can mend
It's well-known to most of us. I call it my "wits' end".

Greetings, Ageless Comrades
When I was young, I wanted to be old
Since then I've reconsidered, so just put that thought on hold.
I have now discovered it was just my wonder
That got up and went, leaving behind its thunder.
Woe is me! It seems my drizzle has reached its fizzle
Could it be I'm dizzy from being in a tizzy?
Woe is me! They say each mind wanders now and then
Funny, I can't remember just where mine has been.
And it seems that while I'm singing my happy tune
I aim too high as if reaching for the moon.
Woe is me! Daily I seek to be wise and witty
Can't seem to get down to the nitty-gritty.
But recently I have felt like a blooper or a blunder
I guess my life has caught up with my wonder.
So there is now a new motto, a new definition of age
Just add the letter *c*; it will then become your cage.
Never let life's challenges form an endless trap
Stand up and protest; give it your best zap.
For the human spirit is our Heavenly Father's design
What is it then that doth now confine?
Signed,
Wonderless

Dieter's Dilemma
Today I rode the diet train as I have many times before
Sitting close to the front, desiring to be near the door.
The same familiar faces I saw among the crowd
Lettuce, celery, and brussels sprouts called my name out loud.
Seated just behind me were the waffles and fries
They are rich and famous much like the cakes and pies.
I tried to ignore them, hoping they'd be quiet
But they like to be included as part of my daily diet.
The hot rolls were in the middle, such luscious and appealing bread
Just how much I love it is yet to be said.
I glanced behind me, and there was the caboose
Is that chocolate hanging there? Oh Lord, turn my spirit loose.
There's quite a battle for those who indulge
Destined to be recorded as the famous "Battle of the Bulge."
Well, time to get off the train, much to my sorrow
But same time, same place, we'll meet again tomorrow.
DDC (Dieter's Dilemma Club)

Dear Friend

Just a note to let you know that I am still alive
Though Heaven only knows how I manage to survive.
Sometimes I falter. I even stub my toe
But I manage to get up again. Just wanted you to know.
I can hear you rooting, "Give it all you've got
You're entering the home stretch. This may be your last shot."
So don't you worry, even though my heart now cries
If this experience doesn't kill me, just think of me as wise!

CONCLUSION

I have shared a brief overview of some of my experiences and what I believe based on the Word of God. Knowing that it is the Word of God that will judge us, it's my desire to walk as close to God as I can and to "live by every word that proceedeth out of the mouth of God" (Matthew 4:4). Also, Galatians 5:25 says, "If we live in the Spirit, let us also walk in the Spirit."

> "The book of the law shall not depart out of thy mouth; but thou shalt meditate therein day and night, that thou mayest observe to do according to all that is written therein; for then thou shalt make thy way prosperous, and then thou shalt have good success".
>
> —Joshua 1:8

> "For I know the thoughts that I think toward you, saith the Lord, thoughts of peace, and not of evil, to give you an expected end".
>
> —Jeremiah 29:11

> "Being confident of this very thing, that he which hath begun a good work in you will be perform it until the day of Jesus Christ".
>
> —Philippians 1:6

> "Then shall we know, if we follow on to know the Lord: his going forth is prepared as the morning: and he shall come unto as the rain, as the latter and former rains unto the earth".
>
> —Hosea 6:3

So, let us continue in the service of the Lord as we anxiously await His soon coming. Remember what Jesus said in Matthew 5:14, "Ye are the light of the world; A city that is set on a hill cannot be hid." Galatians 6:9 says, "And let us not be weary in well doing: for in due season we shall reap, if we faint not." Our Lord will guide us each step of the way.

Each struggle or trial along the way is meant to make us stronger. We could never climb a mountain or encourage someone else without having the strength to do so. There is never a testimony without a test or having been a witness of something to testify about. Second Corinthians 12:10 says, "Therefore I take pleasure in infirmities, in reproaches, in necessities, in persecutions, in distresses for Christ's sake: for when I am weak, then am I strong."

There's nothing like an *experience*. The apostle Paul stated it well in 2 Timothy 1:12: "For

I *know* whom I have believed, and am persuaded that he is able to keep that which I have committed unto him against that day."

"Let us hear the conclusion of the whole matter: Fear God and keep his commandments: For this is the whole duty of man".

—Ecclesiastes 12:13

"For we spend our years as a tale that is told".

—Psalm 90:9

"So teach us to number our days, that we may apply our hearts unto wisdom".

—Psalm 90:12

A Tale that Is Told
When life's final curtain is drawn and I am laid to rest
Will it be said of me,
"She was true to her quest"?
When my days have been numbered and I no longer occupy
When the last chapter is written, its pages all dry.
What picture of my life will then unfold
For we live our lives as *a tale that is told*.

"His Lord said unto him, Well done, good and faithful servant; thou has been faithful over a few things, I will make the ruler over many things: enter thou into the joy of the Lord".

—Matthew 25:23

Let us establish a good report, that of a faithful servant!

To God Be the Glory

Printed in the United States
By Bookmasters